W9-AHZ-783

No Backbone!
The World of Invertebrates

Leaping Grasshoppers

by Meish Goldish

Consultant: Brian V. Brown
Curator, Entomology Section
Natural History Museum of Los Angeles County

BEARPORT
PUBLISHING

NEW YORK, NEW YORK

Credits

Cover, © ahnhuynh/Shutterstock; 4–5, © Stephen Dalton/Minden Pictures; 6, © Jean-Paul Ferrero/Auscape/Minden Pictures; 7, © Stephen Dalton/Minden Pictures; 8, © Anthony Bannister/Animals Animals-Earth Scenes; 9, © Piotr Naskrecki/Minden Pictures; 10–11, © Don Klein/SuperStock; 12, © Stephen Dalton/Minden Pictures; 13, © Mitsuhiko Imamori/Minden Pictures; 14T, © Maximilian Weinzierl/Alamy; 14B, © Dwight Kuhn/Dwight Kuhn Photography; 15, © Charles Krebs/Stone/Getty Images; 16–17, © Harry Fox/Oxford Scientific Films/Photolibrary; 18T, © Dwight Kuhn/Dwight Kuhn Photography; 18B, © Philippe Clement/Nature Picture Library; 19, © Jose B. Ruiz/Nature Picture Library; 20, © OmaPush/iStockphoto; 21, © Kim Taylor/npl/Minden Pictures; 22TL, © Creatas/SuperStock; 22TR, © George Grall/National Geographic/Getty Images; 22BL, © Dmitrijs Mihejevs/Shutterstock; 22BR, © age fotostock/SuperStock; 22Spot, © Andrey Semenov/Shutterstock; 23TL, © Anthony Bannister/Animals Animals-Earth Scenes; 23TR, © Jim Wehtje/Photodisc Green/Getty Images; 23BL, © Don Klein/SuperStock; 23BR, © Charles Krebs/Stone/Getty Images.

Publisher: Kenn Goin
Editorial Director: Adam Siegel
Creative Director: Spencer Brinker
Design: Dawn Beard Creative
Photo Researcher: James O'Connor

Library of Congress Cataloging-in-Publication Data

Goldish, Meish.
 Leaping grasshoppers / by Meish Goldish ; consultant, Brian V. Brown.
    p. cm. — (No backbone! The world of invertebrates)
 Includes bibliographical references and index.
 ISBN-13: 978-1-59716-586-0 (library binding)
 ISBN-10: 1-59716-586-7 (library binding)
 1. Grasshoppers—Juvenile literature. I. Title.

 QL508.A2G65 2008
 595.7'26—dc22
                          2007033952

For more information, write to Bearport Publishing Company, Inc., 101 Fifth Avenue, Suite 6R, New York, New York 10003. Printed in the United States of America.

10 9 8 7 6 5 4 3 2

Contents

Little Leapers

Grasshoppers are **insects** that jump far.

Their back legs are very long and powerful.

A grasshopper can jump 20 times the length of its body.

If people had legs that strong, they could easily hop over two school buses in one jump!

Grasshoppers live and leap in all parts of the world except the North and South Poles.

Strong Bodies

There are about 10,000 different kinds of grasshoppers.

Like all insects, they have six legs and two **antennas**.

Grasshoppers also have a hard covering called an exoskeleton on the outside of their bodies.

The exoskeleton protects the soft parts of a grasshopper's body.

antennas

legs

wings

Most kinds of grasshoppers have wings for flying. They fly or jump when they need to make a quick getaway.

Long-Horned or Short-Horned

Grasshoppers use their antennas to feel and smell things.

Grasshoppers with long antennas are called long-horned grasshoppers.

Grasshoppers with short antennas are called short-horned grasshoppers.

short-horned grasshopper

long-horned grasshopper

Katydids are one kind of long-horned grasshopper. They make a noise that sounds like the words "Katy did, Katy did."

Making Music

Male grasshoppers are famous for the songs they sing.

Long-horned grasshoppers sing by rubbing their wings together.

Short-horned grasshoppers rub one leg against a wing to make music.

A male's songs attract females and keep other males away.

Grasshoppers have no ears on their heads. They hear with ear-like body parts on or near their legs.

Hungry Hoppers

Most grasshoppers eat plants.

In fields and forests, they eat the leaves of plants that grow wild.

On farms, they dine on corn, cotton, and other crops.

Some short-horned grasshoppers travel together for many miles to find food.

These grasshoppers are called locusts.

locust

Billions of locusts may fly in one giant group. They eat large fields of plants wherever they go.

Eggs and Babies

Many kinds of grasshoppers lay eggs in the fall.

A female may lay more than 100 eggs at a time.

The eggs hatch in the spring.

The babies that come out are called **nymphs**.

They look like tiny adult grasshoppers, but they do not have wings.

grasshopper laying eggs

eggs

14

Grasshopper nymphs eat a lot. In fact, they eat even more food than adults.

nymphs

Growing Up

A grasshopper nymph has an exoskeleton.

This hard covering cannot grow, however.

As the nymph gets bigger, it sheds its old exoskeleton so that a new one can form.

This change is called molting.

After five or six molts, the nymph has become an adult.

old exoskeleton

All Kinds of Enemies

Grasshoppers face many dangers.

Spiders, snakes, mice, and birds hunt and eat them.

Beetles and other insects also feed on grasshoppers.

They eat grasshopper eggs, too.

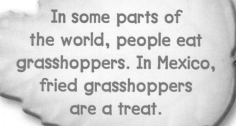

In some parts of the world, people eat grasshoppers. In Mexico, fried grasshoppers are a treat.

Staying Safe

Many grasshoppers escape danger by hopping and flying away.

Some blend in with the colors around them, so enemies can't see them.

Others spit a smelly brown juice at any animal that bothers them.

As long as they stay safe, these insects can keep on leaping!

Many adult grasshoppers live only about 30 days.

A World of Invertebrates

An animal that has a skeleton with a **backbone** inside its body is a *vertebrate* (VUR-tuh-brit). Mammals, birds, fish, reptiles, and amphibians are all vertebrates.

An animal that does not have a skeleton with a backbone inside its body is an *invertebrate* (in-VUR-tuh-brit). More than 95 percent of all kinds of animals on Earth are invertebrates.

Some invertebrates, such as insects and spiders, have hard skeletons—called exoskeletons—outside their bodies. Other invertebrates, such as worms and jellyfish, have soft, squishy bodies with no exoskeletons to protect them.

Here are four insects that are related to grasshoppers. Like all insects, they are invertebrates.

Cricket

Termite

Cockroach

Earwig

Glossary

antennas
(an-TEN-uhz)
the two body parts
on a grasshopper's
head used for
feeling and
smelling

backbone
(BAK-*bohn*)
a group of
connected bones
that run along
the backs of some
animals, such as
dogs, cats, and fish;
also called a spine

insects (IN-sekts)
small animals that
have six legs, three
main body parts,
two antennas, and a
hard covering called
an exoskeleton

nymphs (NIMFS)
young insects
that change into
adults by growing
and shedding their
exoskeleton again
and again

23

Index

Read More

Ashley, Susan.
Grasshoppers. Milwaukee, WI: Weekly Reader Early Learning Library (2004).

Brennan, Patricia.
Grasshoppers and Their Relatives. Chicago: World Book (2003).

Heinrichs, Ann.
Grasshoppers. Mankato, MN: Compass Point Books (2002).

Learn More Online

To learn more about grasshoppers, visit
www.bearportpublishing.com/NoBackbone-Insects

About the Author

Meish Goldish has written more than 100 books for children. He lives in Brooklyn, New York, where he spends much time hopping from library to library.